Launcelot Minor Harris

Studies in the Anglo-Saxon Version of the Gospels

Launcelot Minor Harris

Studies in the Anglo-Saxon Version of the Gospels

ISBN/EAN: 9783743395329

Manufactured in Europe, USA, Canada, Australia, Japa

Cover: Foto ©ninafisch / pixelio.de

Manufactured and distributed by brebook publishing software (www.brebook.com)

Launcelot Minor Harris

Studies in the Anglo-Saxon Version of the Gospels

Studies

in the

Anglo-Saxon Version

of the

Gospels

Part 1 : The Form of the ... ...
... and ... ...

A Dissertation

submitted to the Board of University Studies of
The Johns Hopkins University in ...
degree of Doctor of Philosophy

by

Lawrence ... Harris

1898

There is the case where the context shows a freedom of rendering ~~is that of the all, no strict canon can be~~ ~~laid down & hope in another paper,~~ ~~on the manner~~ ~~of the translation, to make more [?]~~ In the light of ~~an extension~~ exposition of the manner of the translation, which i hope to make in another paper, my reasons for ~~[crossed out]~~ a decision in any given case won in more apparent. Meanwhile I can ~~claim~~ on ~~to have [crossed out]~~ say that I have considered arig in Each instance x

but a decided

To printer. In all cases throughout to page
96 print small letters used to designate
manuscripts in _italics_ ×

Print as follows throughout [All in brevier]: first, the number on right hand margin, [in heavy type] one its index to the other, followed by period; second, The reading of 1st column followed by colon; third, reading of second column followed by colon; fourth reading of third column followed by period and extra space, say ——. Thus:

1st itaque eg: romosttice: ergo.   3.6 abeo in Iordane f DEK q: on iordane fram him: in Iordane abeo.   3.7 ventura W qi futura.
8.25 et accesserunt ad eum discipuli ejus: 7 hig genealachton: et accesserunt.

Note that in Anglo-Saxon æ is a digraph
but in Latin ae two separate letters

Maria

Be careful to omit all passages erased in pencil, and to make the transfers indicated

[illegible]

[illegible]

[illegible]

[illegible]

[illegible]

[illegible]

[illegible]

[illegible]

[illegible]

[illegible]

[illegible]

[illegible]

[illegible]

[illegible] 12 [illegible]

[illegible]

[illegible] 13 [illegible] 13 [illegible]

[illegible]

[illegible]

[illegible]

Assumed Readings

Matthew
(24 readings)

E Q R - - - - - - -	15
L - - - - - -	11
D - - - -	10
Ʒ ⁿᵍ - - -	7
W T - - - - -	5
B θ - - - - -	4
O - - - -	3
C Ʒ T ᶜ - - - - -	2
A H H 'H* H'Ʒ 𝒥 I J	
O'O ˢᵃˣ R ˢᵃˣ V X Xᶜ	
X* Z - - - - -	1

Mark
(12 readings)

1 T O Z - - - -	5
θ Q R - - - -	3
B D E Ʒ H X X G - -	2
A C Ʒⁿᵍ W Y Y'Ʒ -	1

Luke
(19 readings)

Q R - - - -	6
E T - - -	5
C D - - -	4
G - -	3
B Ʒ K Y - -	2
A Ɛ Ɛ ᵃᵉᶜ F I	
J O P W Z* - - -	1

John
(3 readings)

C E T - - - -	2
Ɛ D H I J M θ Q R	
W Z θ - - - -	1

Provable Readings

Matthew
(38 readings)

Q - - - - - - - -	20
R - - - - - - -	18
D E - - - - - -	14
L - - - - - -	13
Ʒ Ʒⁿᵍ O T - - -	5
C Ʒ Y θ - - - -	4
A H* K W - - - -	3
F Hᶜ J M R* V X* Y ᶜ Z - -	2
E* H I T ᶜ X ᶜ - - - -	1

Mark
(24 readings)

1 T - - - -	13
Ɛ L θ - - - -	9
O Q - - - -	8
D - - - -	7
K W - - - -	6
R - - - -	5
C Z - - - -	4
B Ʒ H 'T V V - -	3
A H I X* Y - -	2
Ʒ* Ʒ Ʒᶜ Ʒ'Ʒ⁰	
F M O C - - -	1

Luke
(30 readings)

D R - - - - -	11
K T W - - - -	10
Z - - - -	9
G O Q - - -	8
E - - - - -	7
C F J M T V θ - - -	6
Ɛ X - - - - -	5
B Ʒ H M X* - - -	4
A P - - -	3
I L Z* - - -	2
B'B ᶜ Ʒ ⁿθ H'K*	
O ˢᵃˣ T ᶜ Y - - - -	1

John
(11 readings)

E - - - - - -	8
J R - - - - -	6
D Q T W - - - -	5
C K θ - - - - -	4
B F H S Y Z θ - -	3
A* A G M T V X X* Δ - -	2
G ⁿᵍ K H T ᶜ U	
Y ⁿᵍ Z ᶜ Z² - -	1

C. <u>Character and Types of The</u>
<u>Consultant's Report.</u>

ᶜ		ΛΓ	19
Γ		Ͻ	17
D		Ͽ	15
E		Z	12
L		DǪ	11
B		K	10
Ƒ		ϚL / B	9 / 9
TW		E	8
ƑƏ		RW	7
U		ιT	6
ΣFH		ƷΛΗ	5
AΓIΛ		H	4
ιTγ		Ƒ	3
ᶜ		Aᴦⁱ	2
Ƒⁱⁱᴵᶜⁱ		Ʒˡ⁻ⁱⁱ	1

D 7		D	0
E . 6		E	.
L 10		L	5
q' 4		q'	0
R 11		R	1

9 times in the process.

(ΔήΡΟΥΤΑΣ)

Antecedent meditation

13   17   21   1

          15   22

          17

17   2

                                3

15   20   23

16   24

          21

17   5

From   1891

the College of Charleston, S Carolina.

www.ingramcontent.com/pod-product-compliance
Lightning Source LLC
Chambersburg PA
CBHW051724300426
44115CB00007B/453